WHY?

Questions & Answers

Zeke Wonderly

WELCOME TO WHY? QUESTIONS AND ANSWERS!

Hello, curious explorer! Have you ever wondered why the sky is blue? Or why cats purr? Or even why we yawn (and why it's so contagious)? Well, guess what? You're about to find out!

This book is packed with funny guesses, real answers, and exciting activities to make you think, laugh, and maybe even say, "Whoa! I didn't know that!"

So, grab your thinking cap (or a snack, because learning is hungry work), and get ready to explore the world of WHY!

Let's go on a curiosity adventure!

Are you ready?
Let's ask WHY!

ISBN: 978-1-956369-08-3

WHY IS THE SKY BLUE?

Crayon

Because it lost a bet with the ocean and had to copy its color forever!

Real Answer

The sky looks blue because of a process called Rayleigh scattering.
Sunlight is made of many colors, and blue light is scattered in all directions by tiny molecules in the atmosphere, making the sky appear blue.

Fun Fact

On other planets, the sky can be different colors! Mars has a reddish sky.

Your Mission today!

Go outside and look at the sky—does it look the same shade of blue everywhere?

WHY DO WE HAVE EYEBROWS?

Because our foreheads felt lonely without them.

Real Answer

Eyebrows help keep sweat and rain out of our eyes. They also help us express emotions like surprise and happiness!

Fun Fact

Some people are born without eyebrows and still do just fine!

Task

Try raising one eyebrow at a time in front of a mirror. Can you do it?

WHY DO BIRDS SING?

They're practicing for their world tour—next stop, your backyard!

Real Answer

Birds sing to communicate! They sing to attract mates, warn others of danger, or mark their territory.

Fun Fact

The lyrebird can mimic sounds like chainsaws and car alarms!

Your Mission today!

Try whistling or making bird sounds. Do any birds respond?

WHY DO WE YAWN?

Because our mouths get bored and need to stretch!

Real Answer

Scientists think yawning helps cool down our brains and bring in extra oxygen when we're tired.

Fun Fact

Even animals like dogs and monkeys yawn!

Task

Try making a fake yawn—does it make others yawn too?

WHY DO WE GET GOOSEBUMPS?

Your skin is secretly practicing to become a porcupine.

Real Answer

Goosebumps happen when tiny muscles in our skin tighten, making our hair stand up.
This helped our ancestors stay warm and look bigger when scared!

Fun Fact

Some people get goosebumps when they hear beautiful music!

Your Mission today!

Try rubbing an ice cube on your arm—do goosebumps appear?

Crayon

WHY DO CATS PURR?

They're secretly practicing their DJ skills.

Real Answer

Cats purr when they're happy, but also when they're nervous or trying to heal!
The vibrations may help their bones and muscles recover.

Fun Fact

Big cats like tigers and lions can't purr like house cats!

Task

Try humming in a low voice does it feel like purring?

WHY DO FISH HAVE GILLS?

Because tiny fish scuba tanks are too expensive.

Real Answer

Gills help fish breathe underwater by extracting oxygen from the water.

Fun Fact

Some fish, like lungfish, can breathe air too!

Your Mission today!

Try holding your breath for a few seconds—now imagine living underwater all the time!

WHY DO STARS TWINKLE?

Because they're winking at you!

Real Answer

Stars twinkle because Earth's atmosphere bends their light as it travels to us, making them look like they're flickering.

Fun Fact

If you were in space, stars wouldn't twinkle at all!

Task

Go outside at night and count how many twinkling stars you can see.

WHY IS THE MOON SOMETIMES OUT DURING THE DAY?

The moon forgot to check its schedule.

Real Answer

The moon is always orbiting Earth, and sometimes, its position makes it visible in daylight!

Fun Fact

Astronauts who walked on the moon left their footprints, and they'll stay there for millions of years!

Your Mission today!

Look for the moon during the day—can you find it?

WHY DO ONIONS MAKE US CRY?

Because onions are secretly ninjas attacking your eyes.

Real Answer

When you cut an onion, it releases a gas that mixes with your tears to create a mild acid, which makes your eyes sting.

Fun Fact

Onions were used as medicine in ancient Egypt!

Task

Try putting an onion in the fridge before cutting it does it make a difference?

WHY DO WE GET BRAIN FREEZE?

Because your brain is yelling, "Too cold! Too cold!"

Real Answer

Brain freeze happens when something cold touches the roof of your mouth, making blood vessels quickly tighten and then expand, causing pain.

Fun Fact

The scientific name for brain freeze is sphenopalatine ganglioneuralgia!

Your Mission today!

Try eating ice cream slowly does it stop brain freeze?

WHY DO WE HICCUP?

Your body is playing a drum solo on your lungs.

Real Answer

Hiccups happen when your diaphragm (a muscle that helps you breathe) suddenly tightens, causing a quick intake of air.

Fun Fact

The longest recorded hiccup attack lasted 68 years!

Task

Try holding your breath for a few seconds—does it stop your hiccups?

WHY DO MIRRORS FLIP LEFT AND RIGHT BUT NOT UP AND DOWN?

Because mirrors like playing tricks on us.

Real Answer

Mirrors don't actually flip anything, your brain interprets the reflection that way!

Fun Fact

Some animals, like elephants, can recognize themselves in mirrors!

Your Mission today!

Write a word on a piece of paper and hold it up to a mirror—what happens?

WHY DOES IT RAIN?

The clouds got too full and needed to sneeze!

Real Answer

Rain happens when water from lakes, rivers, and oceans evaporates, forms clouds, and then falls back to Earth when the clouds become too heavy.

Fun Fact

Some places on Earth get almost no rain like the Atacama Desert in Chile, where some areas haven't had rain in 400 years!

Task

Put a glass of water outside in the sun and check later, does any water disappear?

WHY DOES THUNDER MAKE A LOUD NOISE?

It's the sky burping after drinking too much rainwater.

Real Answer

Thunder is caused by the sudden expansion of air when lightning heats it up to five times hotter than the sun! The explosion of heat makes a big boom.

Fun Fact

The longest lightning bolt ever recorded stretched 477 miles across the sky!

Your Mission today!

Count the seconds between a lightning flash and the thunder—every 5 seconds means the storm is about one mile away.

WHY DOES THE WIND BLOW?

Because the air is running late for an important meeting.

Real Answer

Wind happens when warm air rises and cool air rushes in to take its place. This movement of air creates wind!

Fun Fact

The fastest wind ever recorded on Earth was 253 miles per hour during a tropical cyclone!

Task

Blow on your hand, does your breath feel warm or cold? That's wind in action!

WHY DO WE HAVE FINGERPRINTS?

So we don't lose our fingers in a game of hide-and-seek.

Real Answer

Fingerprints help us grip things better! Each person's fingerprints are unique, even identical twins don't have the same ones.

Fun Fact

Koalas also have fingerprints, and they look just like human ones!

Your Mission today!

Press your thumb onto a piece of tape, then stick it onto a dark piece of paper, can you see your fingerprint?

WHY DO WE DREAM?

Because our brains get bored
when we're asleep and want to tell stories.

Real Answer

Scientists think dreaming helps our brains
process emotions, memories, and thoughts
while we sleep.

Fun Fact

Some people have lucid dreams, where they
know they're dreaming and can control what
happens!

Task

Try remembering a dream
when you wake up.
can you write or draw it?

WHY DO WE GET DIZZY WHEN WE SPIN?

Your brain is playing musical chairs with your balance.

Real Answer

Inside your ears are tiny fluid-filled tubes that help you balance. When you spin, the fluid keeps moving, confusing your brain and making you feel dizzy!

Fun Fact

Astronauts train in spinning chairs to help them handle dizziness in space!

Your Mission today!

Spin in a circle for 10 seconds, then try walking in a straight line—can you do it?

WHY DO ZEBRAS HAVE STRIPES?

They couldn't decide between black or white, so they chose both!

Real Answer

Scientists think zebra stripes help them stay cool and confuse predators like lions by making it hard to focus on one zebra.

Fun Fact

No two zebras have the same stripe pattern it's like their fingerprint!

Task

Draw a zebra, but make it any color you want, what would a rainbow zebra look like?

WHY DO DOGS WAG THEIR TAILS?

Crayon

Their tails are practicing for a dancing competition.

Real Answer

Dogs wag their tails to show excitement, happiness, or even nervousness. A fast wag usually means they're happy!

Fun Fact

Some dogs don't wag their tails at all, they express happiness by wiggling their whole bodies!

Your Mission today!

Watch a dog's tail next time you see one,
what mood do you think it's in?

WHY DO BEES MAKE HONEY?

Because they love sweet treats just like us!

Real Answer

Bees make honey from flower nectar to store as food for the colder months when flowers aren't available.

Fun Fact

A single honeybee produces only one-twelfth of a teaspoon of honey in its entire life!

Task

Try tasting a tiny drop of honey, where do you think the bees got the nectar?

WHY DO ASTRONAUTS FLOAT IN SPACE?

Space is a giant trampoline with invisible springs.

Real Answer

Astronauts float because there's very little gravity in space to pull them down like on Earth. They're in freefall, just like when you jump off a diving board!

Fun Fact

Astronauts grow taller in space because there's no gravity compressing their spines!

Your Mission today!

Jump up in the air, imagine if you never came back down

WHY IS MARS RED?

Because it ate too many tomatoes.

Real Answer

Mars is red because its surface is covered in iron-rich dust, which rusts (just like a rusty bike) when exposed to air.

Fun Fact

Scientists think Mars used to have rivers and oceans, but they dried up over millions of years!

Task

Find something rusty, does it look similar to Mars?

WHY DO PLANETS ORBIT THE SUN?

Crayon

Because they don't want to get lost in space.

Real Answer

Planets orbit the sun because of gravity. The sun's strong pull keeps them moving in a circular path, just like how the Earth's gravity keeps us on the ground.

Fun Fact

Jupiter is so big that over 1,300 Earths could fit inside it!

Your Mission today!

Tie a string to a small ball and swing it in circles, this is like a planet orbiting a star!

WHY DO WE HAVE TO SLEEP?

Because our pillows get lonely without us.

Real Answer

Sleep helps our brains organize memories, rest our bodies, and grow. Without sleep, we get tired, forgetful, and cranky!

Fun Fact

Some animals, like dolphins, sleep with only half their brain at a time!

Task

Try staying perfectly still with your eyes closed for 10 seconds—does it feel like sleep?

WHY DO WE SNEEZE?

Our noses love making loud sound effects.

Real Answer

Sneezing is our body's way of getting rid of dust, germs, or tickling sensations in our noses.

Fun Fact

The speed of a sneeze can reach 100 miles per hour!

Your Mission today!

Try holding your nose when you feel a sneeze coming, does it stop?

WHY DO SOCKS DISAPPEAR IN THE WASHING MACHINE?

Sock-eating gremlins live in washing machine

Real Answer

Sometimes small socks get trapped in the machine's filter, slip into hidden spaces, or stick to other clothes.

Fun Fact

There's a scientific name for missing socks: the sock loss index!

Task

Count your socks before and after doing laundry, did they all survive?

WHY DO OUR STOMACHS GROWL WHEN WE'RE HUNGRY?

There's a tiny lion inside your belly practicing its roar.

Real Answer

When your stomach is empty, it squeezes air and fluids, making a growling noise. It's your body's way of saying, "Feed me!"

Fun Fact

Your stomach also growls after eating because it's digesting food!

Your Mission today!

Place your hand on your stomach, can you feel it moving?

Crayon

WHY DOES SPICY FOOD BURN OUR TONGUES?

There's a tiny dragon inside chili peppers breathing fire.

Real Answer

Spicy food contains a chemical called capsaicin, which tricks our nerves into thinking we're feeling heat—even though there's no real fire!

Fun Fact

Birds can eat spicy peppers without feeling any heat at all!

Task

Try drinking milk after eating something spicy, does it help?

WHY DOES CHEWING GUM NEVER DISAPPEAR WHEN WE CHEW IT?

Because it wants to be your best friend forever.

Real Answer

Unlike food, gum is made from a rubbery base that doesn't break down in saliva. That's why we have to spit it out!

Fun Fact

The world's largest bubble gum bubble was 20 inches wide!

Your Mission today!

Try chewing a piece of gum for 10 minutes, does it change texture?

WHY DO RAINBOWS HAVE SO MANY COLORS?

Because nature loves painting the sky!

Real Answer

Rainbows appear when sunlight passes through raindrops, splitting into different colors like a prism.

Fun Fact

No two people see the exact same rainbow because everyone's angle is slightly different!

Task

Use a glass of water and a flashlight can you make a tiny rainbow?

WHY DO OUR EYES ADJUST IN THE DARK?

Because our eyes don't like bumping into furniture.

Real Answer

Our eyes have special cells that help them see in low light by making our pupils bigger.

Fun Fact

Owls can see in almost complete darkness thanks to their huge eyes!

Your Mission today!

Turn off the lights and wait a few minutes, does it get easier to see?

WHY DO WE GET TIRED AFTER EATING?

Because our stomachs are telling us, "Nap time!"

Real Answer

When we eat, blood rushes to our stomachs to help digest food, making us feel sleepy.

Fun Fact

Turkey contains a protein called tryptophan, which makes people extra sleepy!

Task

Try stretching after eating, does it wake you up?

WHY DO WE GET ITCHY?

Your skin is playing a tickle game with you.

Real Answer

Itching happens when something irritates our skin, like dust, bug bites, or dry air. Scratching helps remove the irritation.

Fun Fact

Some people can get itchy just by thinking about it!

Your Mission today!

Try scratching one spot and stopping—does the itch go away or come back?

WHY DO OUR FEET SMELL BAD SOMETIMES?

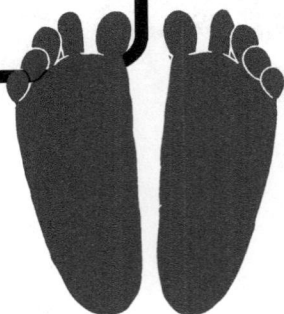

Your feet are sending secret messages to your shoes.

Real Answer

Feet sweat a lot, and bacteria love damp places! When they break down sweat, they create smelly odors.

Fun Fact

Each foot has over 250,000 sweat glands!

Task

Try wearing socks for a whole day, do your feet smell different at night?

WHY DO WE HAVE DIFFERENT TIME ZONES?

So the sun doesn't wake everyone up at the same time!

Real Answer

The Earth rotates, so different places get sunlight at different times. Time zones help us keep track of time across the world.

Fun Fact

Some countries have half-hour time zones instead of full-hour ones!

Your Mission today!

Look up what time it is in another country, how different is it from your time?

WHY DOES METAL FEEL COLDER THAN WOOD?

Metal likes to pretend it lives in the North Pole.

Real Answer

Metal pulls heat away from our skin faster than wood, so it feels colder, even if both are the same temperature!

Fun Fact

Some metals, like mercury, stay liquid even at freezing temperatures!

Task

Touch a metal object and a wooden object, do they feel different?

WHY DOES THE MOON CHANGE SHAPE?

The Moon is playing peek-a-boo.

Real Answer

The Moon doesn't actually change shape, what we see depends on how sunlight hits it as it orbits Earth.

Fun Fact

The Moon is moving about 1.5 inches away from Earth every year!

Your Mission today!

Track the Moon for a week, does it look different each night?

WHY DO WE LAUGH WHEN SOMETHING IS FUNNY?

Our mouths love doing jumping jacks.

Real Answer

Laughing is a brain reaction that releases happy chemicals called endorphins. It also helps us bond with others.

Fun Fact

Babies can start laughing at just 3 months old!

Task

Try forcing a laugh, does it make you feel happier?

WHY DO WE CRY WHEN WE'RE SAD?

Our eyes are cleaning out extra sadness.

Real Answer

Crying helps release stress and signals to others that we need comfort. Our tears even have different chemicals depending on the emotion!

Fun Fact

Some animals, like elephants, cry real tears too!

Your Mission today!

Think of something happy, can you make yourself cry by imagining the opposite?

WHY DO DUCKS FLOAT ON WATER?

They have invisible floaties on their feet.

Real Answer

Ducks have special waterproof feathers and air pockets in their bodies that help them stay afloat

Fun Fact

Ducks can sleep with one eye open to stay safe!

Task

Try placing different objects in water, do they sink or float?

WHY DO OWLS TURN THEIR HEADS SO MUCH?

They're trying to see if someone is sneaking up behind them.

Real Answer

Owls have extra neck bones that let them turn their heads 270 degrees to see all around them.

Fun Fact

Owls can't move their eyes inside their heads like we can!

Your Mission today!

Try turning your head as far as you can, how far does it go?

WHY DO OUR EARS POP IN AIRPLANES?

Our ears are talking to the clouds.

Real Answer

Air pressure changes when planes take off or land, and our ears adjust by "popping" to equalize pressure.

Fun Fact

Astronauts' ears pop a lot because of extreme pressure changes in space!

Task

Try swallowing or chewing gum next time your ears feel funny, does it help?

WHY CAN'T WE TICKLE OURSELVES?

Our brains don't like playing pranks on themselves.

Real Answer

Our brains predict when we try to tickle ourselves, so it doesn't feel surprising, only unexpected touches make us ticklish.

Fun Fact

Some people are more ticklish than others because of their nervous system!

Your Mission today!

Try tickling your own foot, does it work?

WHY DO LEAVES CHANGE COLOR IN THE FALL?

Trees are showing off their new fall fashion.

Real Answer

Leaves contain chlorophyll, which makes them green. In autumn, the chlorophyll fades, revealing red, yellow, and orange colors.

Fun Fact

Some trees turn purple or even pink in the fall!

Task

Some trees turn purple or even pink in the fall!

WHY DOES SAND FEEL HOT ON A SUNNY DAY?

The sand is cooking itself into tiny pancakes.

Real Answer

Sand absorbs heat from the sun very quickly, making it feel hot when we step on it barefoot.

Fun Fact

Some beaches have black, red, or even green sand!

Your Mission today!

Try stepping on sand in the shade, does it feel different?

WHY DO BURPS MAKE NOISE?

Your belly is sending you a secret message.

Real Answer

A burp is just trapped air escaping from your stomach through your throat, making a sound as it rushes out.

Fun Fact

The loudest burp ever recorded was 112 decibels—as loud as a chainsaw!

Task

Try drinking a fizzy drink and see if you burp, does it sound different each time?

WHY DO CLOCKS GO "TICK-TOCK"?

The clock is talking in Morse code.

Real Answer

The ticking sound comes from the gears inside the clock moving at a steady pace to keep time.

Fun Fact

Some clocks, like atomic clocks, are so precise they only lose one second every 15 billion years!

Your Mission today!

Listen to a clock ticking, can you count the seconds?

WHY DO WE SAY "ACHOO!" WHEN WE SNEEZE?

Because sneezes like to introduce themselves.

Real Answer

"Achoo" is the sound our vocal cords make when air rushes out of our nose and mouth at high speed.

Fun Fact

In different languages, sneezes sound different! In Japan, people say "Hakushon!"

Task

Try sneezing with your mouth closed, what sound do you make?

WHY DO OUR FINGERS WRINKLE IN WATER?

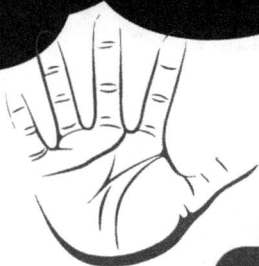

Our fingers are turning into raisins.

Real Answer

Our skin absorbs water, and our nervous system makes it wrinkle to improve grip, like tire treads.

Fun Fact

Scientists believe wrinkly fingers helped our ancestors hold wet objects better!

Your Mission today!

Soak one hand in water and compare it to your dry hand, what's different?

WHY DOES OUR NOSE RUN WHEN IT'S COLD?

Our nose is melting like an ice cream cone.

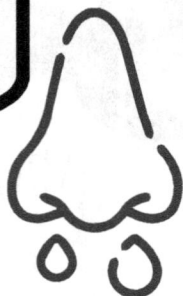

Real Answer

Cold air makes our nose produce extra mucus to warm and moisten the air we breathe.

Fun Fact

Your nose can make up to a pint of mucus per day!

Task

Try breathing through your nose outside, does it start running?

WHY DO BEES BUZZ?

Bees are tiny helicopters.

Real Answer

A bee's wings flap super fast about 200 times per second, creating a buzzing sound.

Fun Fact

Bees can recognize human faces!

Your Mission today!

Try flapping your arms really fast, do you make noise too?

WHY DO WE SEE LIGHTNING BEFORE WE HEAR THUNDER?

Thunder likes to make a dramatic entrance.

Real Answer

Light travels faster than sound, so we see lightning before thunder reaches our ears.

Fun Fact

The longest lightning bolt ever recorded was over 400 miles long!

Task

Count the seconds between lightning and thunder, each second equals about 300 meters away!

WHY DO VOLCANOES ERUPT?

The Earth is burping.

Real Answer

Deep underground, heat melts rock into magma. When pressure builds up, magma explodes out as lava!

Fun Fact

The biggest volcano in the solar system is on Mars!

Your Mission today!

Shake a soda bottle and open it, kind of like a volcano, right?

WHY DO WE YAWN WHEN WE'RE TIRED?

Our mouth is stretching for a workout.

Real Answer

Yawning brings in extra oxygen, cooling the brain and keeping us alert.

Fun Fact

Even dogs and cats yawn when they see humans do it!

Task

Try fake yawning, does it make someone else yawn too?

WHY DO OUR HANDS GET SWEATY WHEN WE'RE NERVOUS?

Our hands are crying.

Real Answer

When we're scared or excited, our body releases adrenaline, which makes our sweat glands work harder.

Fun Fact

Sweat itself doesn't smell, bacteria on our skin create the odor!

Your Mission today!

Try thinking of something scary, do your hands feel different?

WHY DO AIRPLANES STAY IN THE SKY?

Invisible strings hold them up.

Real Answer

Airplanes have special wing shapes that push air downward, creating lift to keep them up.

Fun Fact

The fastest plane ever built flew at 7,273 km/h!

Task

Try making a paper airplane, does it stay up longer with bigger wings?

WHY DO WE HAVE PASSWORDS?

Computers like to play guessing games.

Passwords keep our information safe by making sure only the right person can access it.

Fun Fact

The most common password in the world is "123456"!

Your Mission today!

Try making up a super-secret password, how hard would it be to guess?

WHY DO WE CELEBRATE BIRTHDAYS?

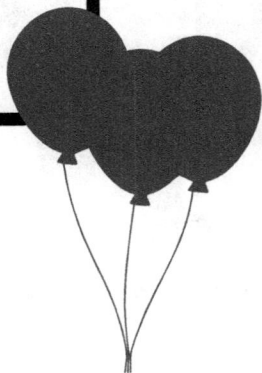

Cake needs an excuse to be eaten.

Real Answer

Birthdays mark the day we were born, and different cultures have special ways to celebrate.

Fun Fact

The song "Happy Birthday" is one of the most-sung songs ever!

Task

Ask someone their birthday, do they celebrate in a special way?

WHY DOES MUSIC MAKE US FEEL THINGS?

Crayon

Our ears like to dance.

Real Answer

Music activates brain areas linked to emotions, memories, and movement.

Fun Fact

Even babies react to music before they can talk!

Your Mission today!

Listen to happy and sad music, do they change your mood?

WHY DO PEOPLE SNORE?

Our nose is playing a trumpet.

Real Answer

Snoring happens when air vibrates in the throat because the muscles relax too much.

Fun Fact

The loudest snore ever recorded was as loud as a lawnmower!

Task

Try breathing through your nose and then your mouth, do you sound different?

WHY DO WE GET SLEEPY AFTER EATING?

Our food is hypnotizing us.

Real Answer

After eating, our body sends more blood to the stomach for digestion, making us feel drowsy.

Fun Fact

Light food don't actually make people sleepy, it's the big meals that do!

Your Mission today!

Eat something heavy and see if you feel sleepy, does it happen every time?

WHY DO LEAVES HAVE VEINS?

Leaves love looking fancy with patterns.

Real Answer

Leaf veins transport water and nutrients, like blood vessels in our body.

Fun Fact

Some leaves are so big, they can be used as umbrellas!

Task

Find a leaf and look at its veins, do they all look the same?

WHY DO WORMS COME OUT WHEN IT RAINS?

They're having a rain dance party.

Real Answer

Worms need moisture to breathe, and rainwater makes it easier for them to move on the surface.

Fun Fact

The longest worm ever found was 22 feet long!

Your Mission today!

After it rains, look for worms outside, where do they go?

WHY DO SOME COLORS LOOK BRIGHTER THAN OTHERS?

Some colors drank extra sunshine.

Real Answer

Some colors reflect more light, making them appear brighter to our eyes.

Fun Fact

Yellow is the easiest color to see from a distance!

Task

Look at different colors in a dark room, do any seem to glow more?

WHY DOES OUR VOICE SOUND DIFFERENT IN RECORDINGS?

The microphone is pranking us.

Real Answer

We hear our voice differently because we hear it both through air and vibrations in our skull.

Fun Fact

Some people dislike their recorded voice because it sounds higher-pitched than they're used to!

Your Mission today!

Record yourself talking, does it sound the way you expect?

WHY DO OUR EARS KEEP GROWING?

They're trying to hear everything in the world.

Real Answer

Unlike bones, our ears are made of cartilage, which continues to grow over time.

Fun Fact

Ears can grow up to 0.22 millimeters every year!

Task

Compare your ears to someone older, do theirs look bigger?

WHY DOES TIME FEEL SLOWER WHEN WE'RE BORED?

The clock is napping.

Real Answer

Our brain processes more details when we're bored, making time feel longer.

Fun Fact

Time flies faster when we're having fun because our brain ignores unimportant details!

Your Mission today!

Try doing nothing for one minute, does it feel like forever?

WHY DO ASTRONAUTS FLOAT IN SPACE?

Space is a giant trampoline.

Real Answer

There's no gravity pulling them down, so they float freely.

Fun Fact

Astronauts grow taller in space because there's no gravity compressing their spine!

Task

Watch videos of astronauts, do they move differently?

WHY DO CAMELS HAVE HUMPS?

It's their built-in backpack.

Real Answer

Camels store fat in their humps, which helps them survive without food or water.

Fun Fact

Camels can drink 40 gallons of water in one go!

Your Mission today!

Try walking without drinking water for a while, how long can you last?

Crayon

WHY DO CHAMELEONS CHANGE COLOR?

They like playing hide-and-seek.

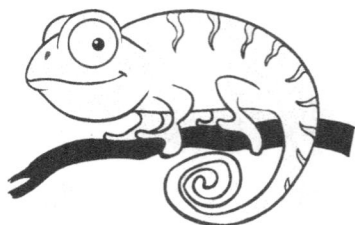

Real Answer

Chameleons change color to communicate, control body temperature, or blend into their surroundings.

Fun Fact

Chameleons don't change color to match backgrounds—they do it based on mood and light!

Task

Look at your clothes, would you blend into your surroundings?

WHY DO DONUTS HAVE HOLES?

Someone took a bite out of every donut ever made.

Real Answer

The hole helps them cook evenly so the center isn't raw.

Fun Fact

The biggest donut ever made weighed 3,739 pounds!

Your Mission today!

Make a donut shape with your hands, does it look tastier?

WHY DO FIREFLIES GLOW?

They swallowed tiny light bulbs.

Real Answer

Fireflies have chemicals in their bodies that produce light through a process called bioluminescence.

Fun Fact

Fireflies flash in different patterns to talk to each other!

Task

Try turning off the lights and watching something glow, what else can glow in the dark?

WHY DOES OUR STOMACH GROWL WHEN WE'RE HUNGRY?

Our stomach is practicing beatboxing.

Real Answer

The muscles in our stomach contract to mix food and gas, making a growling noise when it's empty.

Fun Fact

Stomach growls can happen even when you're not hungry!

Your Mission today!

Try listening closely, can you hear your stomach growling?

WHY DO POPCORN KERNELS POP?

ecause they get too excited when they see a movie!

Real Answer

Inside every popcorn kernel is a tiny drop of water. When the kernel is heated, the water turns into steam, and pressure builds up inside. Eventually, the pressure gets so high that the kernel explodes and turns into the fluffy popcorn we love!

Fun Fact

Popcorn has been eaten for over 5,000 years! Ancient people even used it as decorations for special ceremonies.

Task

Next time you make popcorn, listen carefully, can you hear the tiny pops? Count how many times it pops in a minute!

WHY DO WE LAUGH?

Because our belly likes to do happy little jumps!

Real Answer

Laughter is our brain's way of reacting to funny or happy situations. When we hear a joke or see something silly, our brain releases chemicals that make us feel good. Laughing is also contagious, when we hear someone else laughing, our brain tells us to laugh, too!

Fun Fact

The longest recorded laugh lasted for three hours and six minutes!

Your Mission today!

Try telling someone a funny joke, did they laugh?

WHY DO WE BLUSH?

Because our face wants to turn into a tomato!

Real Answer

Blushing happens when blood rushes to your face due to emotions like embarrassment or excitement. It's controlled by your nervous system!

Fun Fact

Blushing is unique to humans, no other animals do it!

Task

Try thinking about something embarrassing. Does your face feel warm? Check in the mirror!

WHY DO DOGS SNIFF EVERYTHING?

They're reading invisible newspapers!

Real Answer

dog's nose is way more powerful than a human's. They can sniff out tiny details about people, places, and even emotions just from smells!

Fun Fact

Some dogs are trained to sniff out diseases, missing people, and even bedbugs!

Your Mission today!

Hide a snack somewhere and let a dog (or a friend) try to find it using only their sense of smell!

Crayon

WHY DO WE HAVE A BELLY BUTTON?

It's a leftover button from when we were built!

Real Answer

Your belly button is where your umbilical cord was attached when you were in your mother's womb. The cord gave you nutrients before you were born!

Fun Fact

Every belly button is unique! Some are "innies," while others are "outies."

Task

Look at your belly button, what shape is it? Ask a family member if theirs looks the same!

WHY DO BUBBLES POP?

Because they get too full of excitement!

Real Answer

Bubbles are thin layers of soapy water filled with air. When the water evaporates or something touches it, the surface tension breaks, making them pop.

Fun Fact

Bubbles last longer in humid air because they don't dry out as quickly!

Your Mission today!

Try blowing bubbles on a dry, windy day versus a humid day. Do they last longer?

WHY DO SOME PEOPLE HAVE DIMPLES?

Because their cheeks love to smile so much, they made little pockets!

Real Answer

Dimples are caused by small differences in cheek muscles that create indentations when you smile. Some people only have one dimple, while others have two!

Fun Fact

Dimples are actually a genetic trait, meaning they can run in families!

Task

Look in a mirror and smile. Do you have dimples? Check with family members, who has them?

WHY DO BATS SLEEP UPSIDE DOWN?

Because they like hanging out, literally!

Real Answer

Bats sleep upside down because their legs aren't strong enough to support them standing. Hanging also helps them take off quickly when they need to fly!

Fun Fact

Some bats can eat 1,000 mosquitoes in just one hour!

Your Mission today!

Try hanging your head upside down off the couch for a minute, how does it feel?

WHY DO GIRAFFES HAVE LONG NECKS?

Because they want to be the best at hide-and-seek!

Real Answer

Giraffes evolved long necks so they could reach leaves on tall trees and spot predators from far away.

Fun Fact

A giraffe's neck has only seven bones, just like a human's!

Task

Try stretching your neck up like a giraffe—how high can you reach?

WHY DO PEACOCKS HAVE COLORFUL FEATHERS?

Crayon

Because they love showing off their fashion sense!

Real Answer

Male peacocks use their bright feathers to attract mates. The shinier and bigger their tail, the more impressive they look!

Fun Fact

Only male peacocks have colorful feathers, females (peahens) are brown to help them stay camouflaged!

Your Mission today!

Draw your own colorful peacock feathers using crayons or markers, how many colors can you add?

WHY DO ELEPHANTS HAVE BIG EARS?

So they can fly like Dumbo!

Real Answer

Elephants use their big ears to cool down. The large surface area helps release heat, like a built-in fan!

Fun Fact

An elephant's ears can be as big as a car tire!

Task

Try fanning yourself with a piece of paper. Does it cool you down?
Imagine having elephant-sized ears!

WHY DO SOME PEOPLE HAVE FRECKLES?

Because the Sun gives them tiny kisses!

Real Answer

Freckles appear because of extra melanin, the pigment that gives skin color. They become more visible in sunlight!

Fun Fact

Some freckles fade in winter and come back in summer!

Your Mission today!

Stand in the sun for a minute and check your skin, do you have any freckles?

WHY DO SNAKES STICK OUT THEIR TONGUES?

Because they love tasting the air!

Real Answer

Snakes use their tongues to smell the air. They collect scent particles and send them to a special organ in their mouth to understand their surroundings.

Fun Fact

Some snakes can smell better with their tongue than with their nose!

Task

Try sticking out your tongue and wiggling it like a snake. What do you think you could smell if you had super senses?

WHY DO GUMMY BEARS GROW IN WATER?

Crayon

Because they love swimming and eating at the same time!

Real Answer

Gummy bears are made of gelatin, which absorbs water and makes them swell up!

Fun Fact

In salty water, gummy bears shrink instead of growing!

Your Mission today!

Drop a gummy bear in water and check it after a few hours, how much bigger does it get?

WHY DO KANGAROOS HOP INSTEAD OF WALK?

Because walking is too slow for them!

Real Answer

Kangaroos have powerful legs and a big tail that help them hop. Hopping is more energy-efficient for them than walking!

Fun Fact

A kangaroo can jump over 25 feet in one hop, about the length of a bus!

Task

Try hopping across the room, how far can you go in one jump?

WHY DO SOME BIRDS MIGRATE?

Because they want to go on vacation!

Real Answer

Birds migrate to find food and escape cold weather. They follow the seasons to stay in warm places!

Fun Fact

The Arctic Tern travels 44,000 miles every year, the longest migration of any bird!

Your Mission today!

Look outside and spot birds. Do you think they are migratory or do they stay year-round?

WHY DO FROGS CROAK AFTER IT RAINS?

Because they're throwing a rain party!

Real Answer

There's no gravity pulling theFrogs croak after rain because it's the best time to find mates. They need water for their eggs, so they call out loudly when conditions are perfect!m down, so they float freely.

Fun Fact

Some frogs can freeze solid in winter and come back to life in spring!

Task

Try making a frog sound, how loud can you croak?

THE END... OR JUST THE BEGINNING?

Wow! You've just explored so many "Why?" questions—but guess what? The world is FULL of even more amazing mysteries waiting to be discovered!

Science, nature, animals, and even the human body are full of surprises, and every day brings new things to wonder about.
What other "Why?" questions do you have?

Keep the Curiosity Going!
Ask your friends and family a fun "Why?" question, see if they know the answer!
Start your own Why Journal and write down things that make you curious.
Keep exploring, experimenting, and never stop asking why! Remember: Every great scientist, artist, and inventor started with just one question... WHY?

Until next time, keep wondering, keep asking, and keep exploring!

Thank you for reading!

www.ingramcontent.com/pod-product-compliance
Lightning Source LLC
Chambersburg PA
CBHW060404050426
42449CB00009B/1897